C++

The Ultimate Beginners Guide to C++ Programing

Introduction

This book contains proven steps and strategies on how to successfully write programs in C++. It gives you an introduction as well as guides you all throughout the programming language.

This book also contains sample programs and quizzes to help you learn the programming language faster. Likewise, it includes some case studies.

Thank you and I hope you enjoy it!

© **Copyright 2016 by Steve Tale All rights reserved.**

This document is geared towards providing exact and reliable information in regards to the topic and issue covered. The publication is sold with the idea that the publisher is not required to render accounting, officially permitted, or otherwise, qualified services. If advice is necessary, legal or professional, a practiced individual in the profession should be ordered.

- From a Declaration of Principles which was accepted and approved equally by a Committee of the American Bar Association and a Committee of Publishers and Associations.

In no way is it legal to reproduce, duplicate, or transmit any part of this document in either electronic means or in printed format. Recording of this publication is strictly prohibited and any storage of this document is not allowed unless with written permission from the publisher. All rights reserved.

The information provided herein is stated to be truthful and consistent, in that any liability, in terms of inattention or otherwise, by any usage or abuse of any policies, processes, or directions contained within is the solitary and utter responsibility of the recipient reader. Under no circumstances will any legal responsibility or blame be held against the publisher for any reparation, damages, or monetary loss due to the information herein, either directly or indirectly.

Respective authors own all copyrights not held by the publisher.

The information herein is offered for informational purposes solely, and is universal as so. The presentation of the information is without contract or any type of guarantee assurance.

The trademarks that are used are without any consent, and the publication of the trademark is without permission or backing by the trademark owner. All trademarks and brands within this book are for clarifying purposes only and are the owned by the owners themselves, not affiliated with this document.

Table of content

Chapter 1: Introduction to C++ 5

Chapter 2: Getting Started 12

Chapter 3: Programming Fundamentals 21

Chapter 4: Constants and Variables 33

Chapter 5: Operators 40

    Arithmetic Operators 47

    Logical Operators 48

    Bitwise Operators 48

    Misc Operators 49

Chapter 6: Statements and Expressions 51

Chapter 7: Arrays 75

Chapter 8: Case Studies In Terms of Compatibility 87

Chapter 9: Quizzes 91

Conclusion 95

Chapter 1: Introduction to C++

C++ (pronounced *C-plus-plus*) is a general purpose object-oriented programming (OOP) language that is an extension of the C language. If you are familiar with C, you will not have a hard time grasping this language. You can code C++ in an *object-oriented style* or *C style*. In some instances, this programming language may be coded either way. Why is this possible? It is because C++ is also a hybrid language. Furthermore, it's regarded as an intermediate-level language because it encapsulates both low- and high-level language features.

In the real world, C++ is widely used. In fact, it is very common amongst system and application software, client-server applications, embedded firmware, and software drivers. It is practically a collection of pre-defined classes or data types that you can instantiate. It also facilitates user-defined class declaration. You can make the classes accommodate member functions in order to implement functionality. The objects of a certain class can be defined in order to implement functions within a class.

These objects can also be defined as instances that are made during run time. The classes may be inherited by the other classes. They actually take the public in. Plus, they protect functionalities. Moreover, this programming language involves the use of operators such as arithmetic, comparison, logical, and bit manipulation. It allows for the overloading of operators, making it a highly attractive language for programmers.

The essential concepts associated with C++ include virtual functions, friend functions, namespaces, pointers, and polymorphism.

A Brief History of C++

The C++ programming was developed by Bjarne Stroustrup in 1979. During that time, he was using the Stimula language (a language meant for running simulations) to work on his Ph.D. thesis. The Simula 67 was the first language to have supported object-oriented programming. Even though object-oriented programming proved to be highly useful in software development, Stimula was too slow to be used for practical purposes.

Stroustrup then started working on *C with Classes*, which was a superset of the C language. He wanted to incorporate object-oriented programming in C because he found it to be portable, fast, and functional. His language had everything, plus more! Aside from the features found in the C language, he also added basic inheritance, classes, inlining, strong type checking, and default function arguments.

In 1983, C with Classes was changed to C++. The ++ operator was used to increment variables. A lot of new features have also been added to it. Some of these features include virtual functions, function overloading, single-line components, references that use the symbol &, and the keyword *const*.

In 1985, *The C++ Programming Language* was published. Soon enough, C++ became a commercial product. Because it was not yet officially standardized, it became a reference and was updated again in 1989 to feature static and protected members as well as class inheritance.

In 1990, *The Annotated C++ Reference Manual* was released to the public. The Turbo C++ compiler, which was a C++ compiler and integrated development environment developed by Borland, was also released. The Turbo C++ language had an extensive library, which greatly influenced the development of C++. The programming language is still popular and widely used today.

In 1998, the C++ standards committee released the very first C++ ISO/IEC 14882 : 1998 international standard. Eventually, it was called the C++98. It was claimed that *The Annotated C++ Reference Manual* has been a great influence to its development. *The Standard Template Library*, which was conceptually developed in 1979, was included too.

In 2013, the committee released a response to the problems and issues associated with their 1998 standard. When they revised the problems and issues, they also changed its name to C++03.

In 2005, they made a technical report known as TR1, which included details about the features they planned to include in the most recent standard of C++. This latest standard was called C++0x and was originally planned to be released before the decade ended. Sadly, it was only in 2011 when it was finally released to the public.

In 2011, the new standard for C++, called C++11, was finally completed. It was heavily influenced by the Boost library project. Some of its modules were even directly derived from the Boost libraries. Some of the new features include regular expression support, C++ time library, randomization library, atomics support, standard threading library, auto keyword, better union and array-initialization list support, variadic templates, and a new *for loop* syntax.

C++ versus C

Since C++ is newer than C, it definitely has plenty of advantages over the said programming language. It was based on the latter, so it is not surprising that it has retained a lot of its functionality. It did not, however, retain full source-level compatibility. Nonetheless, you will still find many reasons why you should choose C++ over C.

C++ has stronger type checking. It no longer has a void type meant for automatic conversions due to classes and inheritance. It also has type safe linkage. You cannot unknowingly call routines from modules with the use of incorrect arguments, even though your header files are not updated.

You can also take advantage of complex data types, which include all kinds of standard arithmetic operations. Keep in mind that these are used as operators and not as function calls. When you design data types, you can specify which operations or functions you want to use. C++ supports function overloading and user-defined operations.

Additionally, you can use class libraries to have excellent new data types that are easy to use and understand. You can define automatic type conversions when it comes to converting between data types. You can also provide inline functions that combine macros efficiency with function safety. All you have to do is prepend the term *inline* in front of the function so that the compiler can inline it.

Many ANSI C codes are directly compiled by C++. This programming language can actually directly call compiled C codes so that you no longer have to study anything new. There is no need for you to place every declaration on top of every block. Because of this, you are given the freedom to organize your codes into logically-related *paragraphs* that are complete with all the vital declarations.

With this being said, it is much easier to maintain codes. You can quickly and effortlessly move sections of it all around as well as take whatever declaration you feel is necessary. If you use *const*, you can make sure that the variables have their values calculated prior to being changed.

In addition, the classes in C++ have extensible types. They also promote the reuse of codes, so they are able to have a lot of savings on how much code they have written. Take a look, for instance, at an operating system that only has over two hundred thousand lines of code when created in C++. The same operating system is most likely to have over four million lines of code if created in the C language.

C++ versus Java

You may have noticed that the syntax of C++ and Java are very similar. Both programming languages were actually derived from C++. Yes, that is how influential and powerful C++ is. It is an inspiration to a lot of programming languages. Then again, there are still plenty of differences between C++ and Java. Such differences are meant to be huge improvements though. They can also be traced back to their heritage.

C++ and Java actually differ when it comes to their design objectives. C++ was specifically designed for infrastructure programming or systems and applications programming. It was basically an extension of C. It just included support for exception handling, statically-typed object-oriented programming, lifetime-based resource management, template metaprogramming, and generic programming. It also included a standard library that has generic containers, algorithms, and other generic facilities.

Java is a general-purpose, class-based, and object-oriented computer programming language that was specifically designed to have little to new implementation dependencies. It relies on a Java virtual machine for security and portability purposes. It has a vast collection or library that offers a total abstraction of its platform. Moreover, it features Javadoc, which functions as its documentation system.

As a programmer, you may wonder why a lot of people prefer C++ over Java. Well, it's mainly because they find the hypertable to be both memory and CPU intensive.

The hypertable caches the updates in the in-memory data structures. From time to time, such in-memory data structures are spilled into a disk. These files are merged together so that larger files can be formed when their number reaches a particular threshold.

A system's performance relies heavily on the size of its memory. Simply put, the more memory it has, the less merging and spilling occurs. This is a good thing because if the system's memory is smaller, there would be more merging and spilling, which increases the load on the underlying DFS and network. The less memory there is, the more the CPU also has to work.

Java is not recommended for applications that need to use a lot of memory. This is because its memory performance is not as good as that of C++. This is precisely why it is not a good option for managing large in-memory maps of key and value pairs.

There are plenty of places in which the hypertable can be said as CPU intensive. For example, they can be described that way in the in-memory maps of the key and value pairs. Managing and traversing these maps tend to consume a lot of CPU power. The processor caches also tend to be less effective due to the inefficient memory use of Java in regard to such maps. It is possible to do a considerable amount of work in a hundred-and-fifty clock cycles.

In addition, you can say that the hypertable is CPU intensive in the compression. This occurs because all the data you put into the hypertable is compressed two times or more, with three times on average. It is compressed once when you write data on the commit log, another time when you do a minor compaction, and a last time when you perform merging or any major compaction.

How much decompression occurs depends on how much query workload there is available. It can be said that the native

Java implementation of zlib is similar to the implementation of C. From the time you start to experiment with the various compression techniques available, you get to realize that it is necessary to have them implemented in Java. When this happens, however, you will get poor performance. If you choose to use JNI, you will notice that the advantages of Java become pointless and invoking a process through JNI results in a significant overhead.

With regard to the MapReduce Framework and the Hadoop Distributed File System (DFS), it is a known fact that the work done by the MapReduce Framework and the Hadoop Distributed File System is I/O. Hence, you may use Java for these applications. Just remember that some places are sub-optimal for Java. In the DFS's Namenode, for example, there tends to be so much memory pressure. With this being said, you can conclude that Java is not ideal to be used on such applications. It uses up so much memory. It is also sub-optimal when you perform post-map sorting because you get ready for a reduced phase. This makes it CPU intensive, as well as requires CPU work that Java cannot do.

Chapter 2: Getting Started

If you have just started programming, you may find yourself asking a lot of questions. For starters, you may wonder if it is necessary to learn the language beforehand. Well, you will have an advantage if you already know the language, but you will still do well even if you don't. Beginners should not feel compelled to study it. It is alright if they have no previous knowledge of any programming language. This may actually be an advantage because you get to start with a clean slate.

How to Write Programs

C++ is quite demanding in terms of program design. Before you can write a program, you have to design it first. There are simple problems that you can do and practice on as a beginner. As time passes by, however, you will encounter programs that are more complex and these will help you grow. Even though they may give you a headache, they still help you get better at programming by testing your skills and encouraging you to learn more.

What makes a program good? Well, a good program can solve the problem it is meant to solve. It is able to solve it at the right time and on the right budget. A good program design is also free from bugs. This means that you should not encounter an error every time you run it. It should be easy to maintain, so you do not waste time and money on it. Statistics show that 90% of the costs involved in programs are related to maintenance and debugging.

When you first get ready to design a program, you need to ask yourself what problem you are actually trying to solve. Every program has to have a specific goal that is clear and articulated properly. Then, you need to ask yourself if you can really accomplish such task without the need to use custom software.

Oftentimes, it is much better to buy a software program that is already made than to create a new one.

Programmers like to use their time wisely and they are aware that creating something new from scratch will take a huge fraction of their time, as well as require them to exert a lot of effort. So, as a programmer, you have to use resources that you already have on hand. Keep in mind that the programmers who are able to find alternatives to brand new solutions never lose work. You should always be able to find solutions that are inexpensive but also effective.

How about if your problem requires you to create a new program? Before you create one, make sure that you really understand the problem. You cannot provide a solution to a problem that you do not completely understand. You need to examine it carefully and think of the possible solutions. When you are confident that you know what you need to do, you can start creating the design.

The Development Environment

If your computer features a mode wherein you can directly write to its screen, you will have it easy when it comes to graphical environment. It is recommended that you use a graphical environment in Macintosh or Windows. Some users also use compilers that feature text editors built into the system. Others use text editors or word processors that create text files. Then, again, whatever you choose to write your programs in, you should be able to save it in plain text files. In other words, it should not have word processing commands in its text.

You are allowed to use Windows Notepad, Brief, EMACS, vi, Epsilon, and the DOS Edit command among other safe editors. You can also use commercial word processors like Word and WordPerfect. The files you make using editors will be referred to as source files. In C++, they usually come with a *.c*, *.cp*, or *.cpp* extension. You may want to check out your compiler and find out what extension it uses for your source code files.

Always remember that most of the C++ compilers do not mind the extension that you use for your source codes. However, if you do not specify a particular extension, your source code will be named with a *.cpp* extension by default. This is why you have to make sure that you are on a simple text editor when you make your source codes. You can also use the built-in editor of your compiler. It is not recommended to use a word processor that features special formatting characters for saving.

If you ever use a word processor, you should not forget to save your file as an ASCII text. You need to save your source code files using the appropriate extension as well as check your documentations for any specifics with regard to your linker and compiler. This is to make sure that you really know how to link and compile your programs properly.

You can search around if you want. You will find out that most of the free and widely used compilers are GNU C/C++ compilers. Then again, you can also get one from Solaris or Hewlett-Packard (HP), whichever is compatible with your operating system.

GNU C/C++ Compiler Installation

UNIX/LINUX Installation

You can use UNIX or Linux to create programs in C++. If you are using any of these operating systems, see to it that you verify the installation of GCC in your system. Simply type in $ *g++ -v* on your command line. You know that you have GCC if you can see the following on your screen:

Using built-in specs.

Target : i386 – redhat – linux
Configured with : . . / configure - - prefix = / usr . . . .
gcc version 4.1.2 20080704 (Red Hat 4.1.2 – 46)

If you do not have GCC installed, you have to install it. You can go to http://gcc.gnu.org/install/. See to it that you follow the instructions carefully, so you will not have any problems during installation.

Mac OS X Installation

If you are on Mac OS X, you can get GCC by downloading an Xcode development environment from the official website of Apple and following the installation procedures. It is really as simple as that.

Windows Installation

If you are on Windows, see to it that you have MinGW installed on your system. You can go to www.mingw.org and then click on the link that redirects to its download page. Make sure that you get the most recent version of the installation program and name it with *MinGW - < version > .exe*.

When you install MinGW, you should not forget to install gcc-c++, gcc-core, MinGW runtime, and binutils. You are free to install more if you want. You should put your MinGW installation's bin subdirectory to the PATH environment variable. This way, you can identify such tools on your command line using their names. Once you have completed the installation process, you can now run g++, gcc, ranlib, ar, and dlltool among other GNU tools.

Source Code Compilation

Even if your source codes are cryptic and not easy to understand, they should still be *human-readable*. Remember that a source code file and a program are not the same, so it cannot be run or executed like one. If you wish to change a source code and make it a program, you have to use a compiler. The way you invoke this compiler as well as how you command it to search for your source code varies from one compiler to another.

In C++, you have to choose *RUN* or type in *tc < filename >* on this command line. Here, *< filename >* is your source code file's name. You may get a different result if you use another compiler. Once the source code has been compiled, you get an object file, which usually has a *.obj* extension. Then again, remember that it is not possible to execute this program. If you wish to execute it, you have to run the linker.

Creating Executable Files

You can create a C++ program by linking at least one OBJ file with one library or more. The library generally contains linkable files that come with the compiler. Either you have purchased it separately or you produced and compiled it. Take note that all C++ compilers feature a vast library full of procedures or functions. They also have classes that may be included in the program. Functions are blocks of codes that perform a specific function, such as printing to screen or adding numbers. Classes are collections of data and other functions related to it.

When it comes to creating executable files, you need to follow the correct steps. First, you need to make a source code file, using .cpp as its extension. Then, you have to compile your source code into a file. Use .obj as its extension. Finally, you have to link this OBJ file using the necessary libraries in order to produce your executable program. These three steps are crucial, so do not ever forget them.

The Development Cycle

You can have a complete development cycle when your program successfully produces your desired output on your first try. Just write your program and compile the source code. Then, you have to link this program before you run it. Then again, some programs do not let you achieve your objectives.

Some programs contain bugs or errors, which is why you have to check your code carefully. There are bugs that can cause a failed compile or link. Others may only appear once you started running the program. When you find a bug, no matter what type or category it belongs to, you have to fix it immediately. You have to edit the source code right away. You need to recompile, relink, and rerun your program.

Simple Programs

'Hello World' is the most commonly used phrase in programs. It is actually very easy to use. Just type it in your editor and then save, compile, link, and run it. If the program is successful, you will see 'Hello World' printed in your screen.

Here is how your program should look like:

```
1 : #include < iostream.h >
2 :
3 : int main ( )
4 : {
5 : cout << " Hello World! \n " ;
6 : return 0 ;
7 : }
```

Always pay attention to your punctuations. As you can see on the fifth line, the redirection symbol (<<) is used. You can input it by holding the Shift key on your keyboard and pressing the comma key two times. Remember that you should end your code with a semicolon (;). Otherwise, your program will not run.

See to it that you follow the compiler directions properly. Many compilers link automatically, but you should still check your documentation to verify things. In case you get an error, check your code again and find out if you forgot to include something.

If you encounter an error on the first line like *cannot find file iostream.h*, you should view the compiler documentation and search for directions on how you can set up the environment variables or *include* path. If you see an error that says you do not have a prototype for *main*, you should type in *int main ( ) ;* right before the third line. You need to include this line before the start of your *main* function. Most compilers do not really require it, but some still do.

This is what your program should look like:

```
1 : #include < iostream.h >
2 :
3 :
4 : int main ( ) ;
5 : {
6 : cout << " Hello World! \n " ;
7 : return 0 ;
8 : }
```

If you run HELLO.EXE, you would get the following output:

Hello World!

Compile Errors

There are many different reasons why compile-time errors occur. More often than not, they are merely caused by typographical errors or any other minor errors. A good compiler will not just tell you whatever you did that is wrong. It will also direct you to the erroneous area in your code.

The easiest way on how to find out if there are errors in your program is to intentionally include an error in it. For example, you used HELLO.CPP and it was successful. You can edit it and remove your closing brace on the sixth line. Then, you have to recompile the program. You should get an error that is similar to this:

Hello.cpp, line 5 : Compound statement missing terminating } in function main ( ) .

When you see it, you should realize what the problem or issue is. Error messages generally tell you the problem's file and line number. In this case, your problem is on the fifth line because the error message says so. Your compiler is not sure whether or not you really intended to place your closing brace before or after *cout*. There are times when errors only direct you to the general area of the problem or issue. If your compiler is capable of identifying all problems and issues, it can fix your code on its own.

Text Editor versus Word Processor

There is a difference between the text editor and the word processor that many users are not aware of. The text editor produces files that contain plain text. You are not allowed to use anything else other than plain text. The word processor, on the other hand, does not have any restrictions when it comes to special symbols and formatting commands. You can use text files, and they do not have an automatic bold print, word wrap, and italics among others.

Using the Built-In Editor of the Compiler

Compilers compile codes from the text editor. When you use the built-in text editor, you can move back and forth quickly between the compile and edit steps of your development cycle. Complex compilers generally have a development environment that is fully integrated. This allows you to access any help files as well as compile and edit codes. It also lets you resolve link and compile errors without having to leave the development environment.

Ignoring Warning Messages

When you see warning messages pop up on your computer, you have the option to either ignore them or attend to them. Most of the time, nothing really bad will happen if you ignore them. Nonetheless, it is still best if you would be wary of such warnings. If you see one, you should treat it as if it was an error. C++ compilers tend to warn users whenever they do something unintentionally. When you find out what these warning messages are about, you need to take the necessary action.

Compile Time versus Link Time versus Run Time

Compile time is the time you run the compiler while link time is the time you run the linker. Run time, on the other hand, is the time you run the program. As a programmer, you have to familiarize yourself with this shorthand so you can do your work quickly and efficiently.

Chapter 3: Programming Fundamentals

C++ programs usually consist of objects that communicate through the invoking of their methods. They feature objects, classes, methods, and instant variables. An object has behaviors and states. A class tells about an object's behaviors and states. A method is a behavior. There can be various methods in a class. These methods are where data are manipulated, actions are executed, and logics are created. The state of an object is developed by the values allocated to the instant variables.

Structure of a Program

The following are the different parts of a program.

```
#include < iostream >
using namespace std ;
// The program starts to execute at main ( ).
int main ( )
{
cout << " Hello World " ;          // This line prints Hello World
return 0 ;
}
```

You can see that there are headers containing information or data. In the given example, the header < *iostream*> is used. The line in which *using namespace std ;* was written instructs your compiler to make use of the std namespace.

In the succeeding line, a single-line comment is written. Single-line comments start with // . This signifies that that particular line is meant for a comment or note. Comments are important in programs because they serve as reminders as well as improve the readability of the program. You can use comments to organize your codes better, so you will not be confused and commit a lot of errors.

You can add comments if you know that it will take some time before you complete your program. They will help you remember exactly where you left off, as well as what your previous codes were meant for. Comments are also beneficial to the readers. With comments, they will be able understand the codes better because they will know what the programmer wants to convey.

In this sample program, *int main ( )* is where the program starts to execute. After that line, *cout << " Hello World "* is written. It prompts the phrase " Hello World " to be displayed on your screen. Then, there is the line that contains *return 0 ;* , which terminates the function *main ( )* and prompts it to return *0*, which is your given value, to the calling process.

Cout

It is used if you want to print a certain value on your screen. Do not forget to use the insertion operator (<<). It consists of two characters (the less-than symbol), but C++ still treats it as a single character. You have to enter your data after this character. Take a look at the following example:

```
1 : // This is a cout example.
2 :
3 : #include < iostream.h >
4 : int main ( )
5 : {
6 : cout << " Hey there, what's up? \ n " ;
7 : cout << " This is the number 10 : " << 10 << " \ n " ;
8 : cout << " The endl is a manipulator and it writes another line to your screen. " << endl ;
9 : cout << " This is a huge number : \ t " << 10000 << endl ;
```

```
10 : cout << " This is the sum of 2 and 3 : \ t " << 2 + 3 << endl;
11 : cout << " This is an example of a fraction : \ t \ t " << ( float ) 1/3 << endl ;
12 : cout << " This is an example of a really huge number : \ t " << ( double ) 5000 * 5000 << endl ;
13 : cout << " My name is Wendy! \ n " ;
14 : cout << " I am an engineer and a master programmer. \ n " ;
15 : return 0 ;
16 : }
```

If you run the code shown above, you will get the following output:

```
Hey there, what's up?
This is the number 10 : 10
The endl is a manipulator and it writes another line to your screen.
This is a huge number : 10000
This is the sum of 2 and 3 : 5
This is an example of a fraction : 0.333333
This is an example of a really huge number : 2.5e+07
My name is Wendy!
I am an engineer and a master programmer.
```

Using the output of the program, you have to analyze the structure, one line at a time.

On the third line, you can see *#include < iostream.h >*. The file *iostream.h* was added to the source code. If you are using *cout* and other related functions, it is necessary for you to use it.

On the sixth line, the command cout was used in its simplest sense; thereby, printing a series or string of characters. The \ n symbol is actually a special formatting character that commands cout to print a newline character.

On the seventh line, three values are passed to cout. An insertion operator separated each one of the three values. Your first value is a string. You wrote " This is the number 10 : " . Take note that the space found after the colon is still part of your string. The value 10 is then passed onto the newline character and your insertion operator. You can get the output when you use single quotes or double quotes.

> This is the number 10 : 10

This output gets printed on your screen. Since there are no newline characters that follow the first string, the next value is printed. When this happens, the process of concatenation is done. The two values have just been concatenated.

On the eighth line, you gave out a valuable message about endl and you had it printed on your screen. It is crucial to put endl at the end in order for a new line to appear.

On the ninth line, you introduced \ t , which is another formatting character. Its main purpose is to insert a tab character. It is present in lines 9 to 12. It has to be there to line up their output. On the ninth line, integers are not the only ones that can be displayed, but long integers as well.

On the tenth line, you performed addition. It is a basic math procedure. You used the values 2 and 3. Adding them up results in the new value 5, which is shown in your output. The value of 2 + 3 is passed on to cout, which is why 5 is printed and displayed.

On the eleventh line, you passed the value 1/3 onto cout. Since you wanted such value to be evaluated as a decimal equivalent, you used *float*. This term causes cout to print out a fraction.

On the twelfth line, you passed the value 5000 * 5000 onto cout. You used *double* to indicate that you wanted a scientific notation to be displayed.

On the fourteenth line, you gave out some information about yourself and such information was printed to your screen.

Comments

Writing a program requires you to be careful and articulate. A messy program does not only cause errors, but it also results in confusion. If you have been working on a particular program for so long, you may tend to forget some details. This is why you have to take down notes.

Comments in programs seem to be unnecessary lines. However, they are actually needed because they help bring clarity and organization to your program. Without them, your program may be unclear and confusing. If you, yourself, cannot remember the details and understand your own program, how can you expect other people to understand it? The comments in C++ are merely texts that your system ignores. So, you can write anything in your comments sections.

Comment Types

In general, comments are divided into two categories: double – slash (//) and slash – star (/*).

Double – slash comments, also known as C++ - style comments, tell your compiler to refrain from minding the things that follow them. Whatever you write after this comment, the compiler ignores. This goes on until it reaches the end of that particular line.

Slash – star comments, also known as C – style comments, tell your compiler to refrain from minding the things that follow them. Whatever you write after the star – slash (*/) comment mark is not read by your computer. Always remember that each /* has to be paired with a closing */ .

In the C language, the C – style comment is also used. However, the C++ - style comment is not really a part of it. A lot of C++ programmers prefer to use the C++ - style comment in their work and only turn to the C – style comment to block out huge blocks in their program.

Using Comments

As a programmer, you are advised to put comments at the start of your programs so that you can clearly define what these programs do. The moment you read a program, you should immediately be able to tell what its main purpose is. You should also be informed about its author as well as the date it was created. Likewise, you should know about the functions used in the program.

The statements that are not that obvious must include comments so they can be noticed more easily. You should remember that comments do not really affect your programs. When you run your code, the process and the output stay the same. Thus, you should not worry too much about creating perfect comments.

To help you understand comments better, take a look at the following example:

```
1 : #include < iostream.h >
2 :
3 : int main ( )
4 : {
5 : /* This is an example of a comment
6 : that extends to the next line
7 : and to the line after that. */
8 : cout << " Hi Wendy Dawn! \ n " ;
```

9 : // This is an example of a comment that ends when the end of the line is reached
10 : cout << " Good morning beautiful! \ n " ;
11 :
12 : // This shows that you can use a double slash comment
13 : /* This one shows that you can use a slash – star comment */
14 : return 0 ;
15 : }

If you run the above given example, you will get the following output:

Hi Wendy Dawn!
Good morning beautiful!

As you can see in the program, the compiler ignored the comments on lines 5 to 7. Likewise, it ignored the comments written on the ninth, twelfth, and thirteenth lines. The comment you wrote on the ninth line ended when the end of the line was reached. Then again, the comments you wrote on the fifth and thirteenth lines required closing comment marks.

Comments Seen at the Top of Every File

Ideally, you should include a comment block at the start of each file you create. Their style depends on your personal preference though. So, you should feel free to tweak your programs in any way that you think is appropriate. Nevertheless, you have to make sure that your headers include the following:

- The name of your program or function
- The name of your file
- The purpose of your program or function
- A description or summary explaining how your program works

- Your name, if you are the author of the program
- A history of your revisions, including the notes you made on all changes
- The liners, compilers, and other tools you used to create your program
- Any other additional notes

It is very important to keep descriptions and notes updated. Do not make the mistake that a lot of programmers do. They tend to neglect the comments section once they are done with their programs. They think that it is okay to leave the comments since the program is already working.

Once you complete your program, see to it that you still check their headers. If you neglect these headers, the program becomes misleading over time. Readers get confused because they are not aware that the headers are not up to date. You have to keep in mind that comments can serve as invaluable guidelines to your overall program only if they are properly maintained. See to it that you re-visit your program once in a while and update its header.

Functions

The function *main ( )* is unusual yet important in the C++ programming language. Throughout the program, you have to call or invoke functions. Your program is executed one line at a time. It follows the order in which it is written in the source code. This continues to occur until a particular function is reached. Afterwards, your program attempts to execute such function. Once successful, the function gives the control back to the line of code that immediately follows the function call.

Demonstrating Function Calls

To understand functions better, take a look at the following sample program:

```
1 : #include < iostream.h >
2 :
3 : // This shows the function Sample Function
4 : // This prints out a message that you have selected
5 : void SampleFunction ( )
6 : {
7 : cout << " In Sample Function\ n " ;
8 : }
9 :
10 : // This shows that the function main displays a message before
11 : // calling out SampleFunction and printing out
12 : // another message
13: int main ( )
14: {
15: cout << " At main \ n " ;
16 : SampleFunction ( ) ;
17 : cout << Return to main \ n " ;
18 : return 0 ;
19 : }
```

If you run the sample program shown above, you will get the following output:

At main
In Sample Function
Return to main

As you can see, the function SampleFunction ( ) has been defined on the fifth, sixth, and seventh lines. When it is called, it prints out a message to your screen and returns it. However, the actual program does not really begin until the thirteenth line. On the fifteenth line, main ( ) displays a message that says it is in main ( ).

Once this message has been printed out, the sixteenth line calls SampleFunction ( ). Because of this, the commands at SampleFunction ( ) are executed. Take note that your functions consist of the code that you have on the seventh line, which in turn displays a different message.

Once SampleFunction ( ) has been completed, it goes back to where it was first called. Still referring to the sample program shown above, it goes back to the seventeenth line, wherein main ( ) prints out the last line.

Functions either return void or return a value. When a function returns void, it does not return anything. A function that adds a couple of integers may return their sum, thereby returning an integer value. A function that only prints out a message does not have anything to return and is called to return void.

In general, functions feature a body and a header. The header consists of the function name, return type, and parameters associated with that particular function. The parameters of the function allow the values to be passed onto a function. Hence, if the function was to sum up two numbers, these numbers will be the parameters to that specific function.

The following is an example of a function header:

```
int sum ( int y , int z )
```

Parameters are declarations of the types of values that you intend to pass in. Arguments are the actual values passed in by your calling function. A lot of programmers make use of these terms and treat them the same. However, you can also treat them with a distinction.

The body of the function consists of opening and closing braces as well as a statement. You can use as many statements as you want. Conversely, you can use zero statements. As long as you still follow the correct syntax, you can skip using a statement.

Statements constitute the work of the function, which may return a value through the return statement. This statement also causes a function to exit. If you do not place a return statement into the function, it automatically returns void at its end. Such value has to be a type that is declared in your function header.

The #include

The word #include is never absent in a working program. It is a directive to the preprocessor. For every time you call on to your compiler, your preprocessor runs. The #include directive causes whatever file you name after it to be read as if it was typed in at that particular location in the source code.

The // Comment versus the /* Style comment

When it comes to comments, you can choose between these two. They are different from each other though. The double – slash comment (//) expires by the end of the line while the slash – star (/*) comment stays in effect until the closing comment (*/) is reached. The slash – star comment cannot be terminated that easily. Even when it reaches the end of the line, it may still continue until you place a closing comment mark. If you do not put this particular comment mark, you will encounter a compile – time error.

Bad Comments versus Good Comments

It should not really be difficult for you to tell apart bad comments from good comments. A bad comment only restates the function of the code. It states what is already obvious and you can eliminate it without experiencing any problems with your program. You know that the comment is bad when you read the line of code and you already get its point, including what it is, what it does, and why it does it. A good comment, on the other hand, tells you why such code does whatever it does. It also explains what that particular code section is about.

Chapter 4: Constants and Variables

Your program has to store the data that it uses. Constants and variables have different ways of representing and manipulating data.

Defining Variables

A variable is where you store your program information. It is found in the memory of your computer. Here, you can store values that you can retrieve later on.

The name of your variable is a label. For instance, you can use the variable name myVariable. How many memory addresses there are depends on how big your variable name is.

RAM, on the other hand, stands for random access memory. Every time you run a program, it gets loaded from a disk file to a RAM. Every variable is also made in the RAM. In programming, memory is typically used to refer to the RAM of a computer.

Setting the Memory Aside

When you define a variable, you have to inform your compiler about the type of variable you used. You have to state if it is an integer or a character. You have to tell your compiler because such information becomes the basis for determining how much room you have to reserve and what type of value you can use to store your variable in.

The type of variable that you use tells your compiler how much memory it has to reserve for such variable. Since computers make use of bytes and bits when it comes to representing values, and since memory is usually measured in bytes, you have to take note of these concepts very carefully.

Integer Sizes

Every type of variable takes up a specific room amount. For example, an integer may be three bytes on a certain machine and three on another, but never changes when it is on either computer.

You can use the variable *char* to hold or store characters. Usually, it is a byte long, while a short integer is a couple of bytes long. A *long* integer, on the other hand, tends to be four bytes, while an integer that does not have the keywords *long* or *short* may be two or four bytes.

You should also learn about *character*, which takes up a byte of your computer's memory. It is usually a letter, symbol, or number.

Take a look at the following sample program. It determines the size of your variable type.

1 : #include < iostream.h >
2 :
3 : int main ( )
4 : {
5 : cout << " This is the size of the int : \t \t " << sizeof (int) << " bytes . \n ";
6 : cout << " This is the size of the short int : \t " << sizeof (short) << " bytes . \n ";
7 : cout << " This is the size of the long int : \t " << sizeof (long) << " bytes . \n ";
8 : cout << " This is the size of the char : \t \t " << sizeof (char) << " bytes . \n ";
9 : cout << " This is the size of the float : \t \t " << sizeof (float) << " bytes . \n ";

10 : cout << " This is the size of the double : \t \t " << sizeof (double) << " bytes . \n " ;
11 :
12 : return 0 ;
13 : }

If you run the sample program shown above, you will get the following output:

This is the size of the int : 2 bytes .
This is the size of the short int : 2 bytes .
This is the size of the long int : 4 bytes .
This is the size of the char : 1 bytes .
This is the size of the float : 4 bytes .
This is the size of the double : 8 bytes .

It is okay if the number of bytes is different on your screen. Do not panic because every computer is different. The example only shows you the possible output that you can get when you run the sample code.

You may have also noticed that the function *sizeof ( )* was used all throughout the fifth to the tenth lines. Your compiler provides this function, and it informs you of the size of the object that you pass in as parameter. Consider the fifth line. Here, *int* was passed onto *sizeof ( )*. When you use *sizeof ( )*, you will find it much faster and easier to identify that *int* has the same number of bytes as *short int*.

Signed and Unsigned Integers

Integers are either signed or unsigned. You may need negative values at certain times, so you have to know what type of integer you need. Integers are generally assumed to be *signed*, unless they contain the word *unsigned*. This applies to both long and short integers.

Signed integers are either positive or negative. Unsigned integers, on the other hand, are always positive. Unsigned short integers have the capacity to handle numbers between 0 and 65,535. Half of the numbers represented by signed short integers are negative. Signed short integers only have the capacity to represent numbers between -32,768 and 32,767.

Basic Variable Types

There are other variable types in the C++ programming language. These variable types may be divided conveniently into integer variables, character variables, and floating point variables. Floating point variables contain values that are allowed to be expressed as fractions. However, this is only possible if they are real numbers. Character variables can also contain just one byte. They are typically used for holding the two hundred and fifty-six symbols and characters of ASCII and its extended character sets.

The *ASCII character set* is a set of characters standardized to be used on computers. If you still do not know what ASCII stands for, it's American Standard Code for Information Interchange. Almost all computer operating systems support ASCII, and many of them support international character sets.

The variable types typically used in programs are written as follows. Here, you will see the variable type and how much memory it takes up. You will also learn about the types of values that these variables can store. These values can be stored and determined through the size of their variable types.

Type	*Size*	*Values*

unsigned short int	2 bytes	0 to 65,535
short int	2 bytes	-32,768 to 32,767
unsigned long int	4 bytes	0 to 4,294,967,295
long int	4 bytes	-2,147,483,648 to 2,147,483,647
int (16 bit)	2 bytes	-32,768 to 32,767
int (32 bit)	4 bytes	-2,147,483,648 to 2,147,483,647
unsigned int (16 bit)	2 bytes	0 to 65,535
unsigned int (32 bit)	2 bytes	0 to 4,294,967,295
char	1 byte	256 character values
float	4 bytes	1.2e-38 to 3.4e38
double	8 bytes	2.2e-308 to 1.8e308

The sizes of your variables may not be exactly the same as the ones shown in the sample table above. Again, this can be a case to case basis. It depends on the computer and compiler that you have. If you get the same results, then the table applies to the compiler that you use. Otherwise, you should check out the manual of your compiler to see which values are held by your variable types.

Defining Variables

You define or create variables by means of stating the type, following it by at least one space and its variable name, and closing it with a semicolon. For your variable name, you can use any letters. You can combine uppercase with lowercase letters. You can use numbers and combine them with letters for your variable name. However, you should never include a space in your variables.

For example, *w*, *WendyDawn*, *W3ndY*, and *wendyy* are all legitimate variable names. They may seem the same, but they are actually different. Also, even if you can use any variable name you want, make sure that you choose something that is beneficial to your program. Go for a variable name that tells you and your readers what the program is about. For instance, if you are using an integer variable named *myAge :* , you can write it this way:

```
int myAge ;
```

A rule of thumb is to avoid using gibberish names such as *haFihDR93*. You cannot make any sense of this word, and someone is most certainly not named that way. Also, you should avoid restricting your variable names to single letters because they tend to cause confusion even if they are legitimate.

As much as possible, you should use variable names that already give a clue as to what your program is all about. People should know what the program does even before they read the entire code or run the program. Expressive names like *myAge*, *SpeedLimit*, and *howMany* are all easy to understand and direct to the point. When you see these variable names, the first thing that comes to your mind may be to find out the age, speed limit, or number of a particular object in the program.

Take a look at the following example:

```
main ( )
{
unsigned short a ;
unsigned short b ;
ULONG c ;
c = a * b ;
}
```

While it is perfectly clear that the program performs the mathematical operation *multiplication*, as evident in the variable c where the variable a is multiplied to the variable b, it is still unclear what these variables stand for. What exactly do a, b, and c represent? Are they units of measurement? Are they specific values? The lines of code do not make it clear what these variables are about. Therefore, these variable names are not ideal. Seeing this program for the first time may baffle you, especially if you do not have any previous experience with programming.

Take a look at another example:

```
main ( )
{
unsigned short Area ;
unsigned short Length ;
unsigned short Width ;
Area = Length * Width ;
}
```

Referring to the example shown above, it is clear that the variables represent the area, length, and width of a particular object. This program is much easier to comprehend than the previous one. As you can see, the objective of the program is to find the area of a particular object by multiplying the length and width.

Chapter 5: Operators

In this programming language, constants and variables are operated or controlled by the operators. The basic operators are practically the same as arithmetic operators.

These arithmetic operators include the plus sign (+) for performing addition, the asterisk (*) for performing multiplication, the minus sign (-) for performing subtraction, the forward slash symbol (/) for performing division, the percentage sign or the modulus (%) for finding the remainder, and the equal sign (=) for assigning expressions.

There are also other operators used in C++ for additional tasks. For instance, the iostream header lets you use the insertion operator (<<) if you want to process an output. You can also access other operators even without using the #include directive. These basic operators are classified under comparison operators, increment and decrement operators, logical operators, and compound assignment operators.

Variable Declaration

Before you use variables in your operations, make sure that you declare them first. You also have to identify their values. When you declare a variable, you have to use the following syntax:

type variable ;

Do not forget to specify the data type, just like when you initialize functions. So, if you want to declare *w* as an integer variable type, you need to initialize it. You can do that by typing this:

int w ;

Once you are done declaring w, you can allocate a specific value to it, with the use of the assign operator (=). For example, if you want to assign the value *10* to the variable *w*, you should write the following:

w = 10 ;

See to it that you declare the variable prior to assigning it a value. Likewise, you have to declare your variable and allocate a value into it by using just one line. For example:

int w = 10 ;

Other than using these expressions for your program, you may also want to consider using operators.

Increment and Decrement Operators

The increment operator consists of two plus signs (++). The decrement operator consists of two minus signs (- -). The primary purpose of these two operators is to make the expression of adding and subtracting 1 from the variable shorter so that you can save space in your program. You will also spend less time and energy in your code. For instance, you can use the following:

if w = 4 , then + + w must be equal to 5 while - - w must be equal to 3.

You can include the increment and decrement operators as either a suffix or a prefix in your program. You can do this if you want to identify the values of two or more variables. When you use the increment and decrement operators as suffices (x++ or x - -), the original value of x prior to the addition or subtraction of 1 would be denoted. If you run them on their own, both the x++ and the ++x would have a similar meaning. Conversely, if you use it in setting other variables, you would be able to notice that their difference is much obvious.

```
a = 5 ;
b = ++a ;
```

As you can see in the example shown above, the value of b is determined only after the value of a is increased. Thus, the value of b becomes 6.

```
a = 5 ;
```

```
b = a++ ;
```

Still on the same note, you can see that the value of b is determined before the value of a is increased. Thus, the value of b becomes 6.

Compound Assignment Operators

Aside from the standard assignment operator (=) and the basic arithmetic operators, you can also use compound assignment operators to perform operations before you assign values. These operators are practically shortened versions of the usual expressions involved in basic arithmetic operators.

```
x + = 1 ;              // It is practically the same as the
expression x = x + 1 ;

x - = 1 ;              // It is practically the same as the
expression x = x − 1 ;

x * = y ;              // It is practically the same as the
expression x = x * y ;

x /= y ;               // It is practically the same as the
expression x = x / y ;
```

Assignment Operators

Operators	Descriptions
=	It is a simple assignment operator that allocates a value from the right side operand to the left side operand.
+=	It is an add AND assignment operator that adds the right operand and the left operand together, and then allocates the resulting value to the left operand.
-=	It is a subtract AND assignment operator that subtracts the right operand from the left operand, and then allocates the resulting value to the left operand.
*=	It is a multiply AND assignment operator that multiplies the right operand with the left operand, and then allocates the resulting value to the left operand.
/=	It is a divide AND assignment operator that divides the left operand with the right operand, and then allocates the resulting value to the left operand.

%=	It is a modulus AND assignment operator that takes the modulus by using two operands and assigning the resulting value to the left operand.
<<=	It is a left shift AND assignment operator.
>>=	It is a right shift AND assignment operator.
&=	It is a bitwise AND assignment operator.
^=	It is a bitwise exclusive OR and assignment operator.
|=	It is a bitwise inclusive OR and assignment operator.

Comparison Operators

You can use comparison or relational operators to compare variables and expressions. These operators can help you verify whether or not a particular value is less than, greater than, or equal to another.

Operators	*Descriptions*

==	It verifies if the values are equal.
!=	It verifies if the values are not equal.
>	It verifies if the value of the first is greater than that of the second.
<	It verifies if the value of the first is less than that of the second.
>=	It verifies if the value of the first is greater than or equal to that of the second.
<=	It verifies if the value of the first is less than or equal to that of the second.

Comparison operators are often used to write condition statements. You can also use them to evaluate expressions and return Boolean values. Referring to the comparison operators in the table shown above, the following are sample expressions with their respective Boolean values:

(8 == 1)   // This line evaluates to "false"
(8 != 1)   // This line evaluates to "true"
(8 > 1)   // This line evaluates to "true"
(8 <= 1)   // This line evaluates to "false"

As you can see, the Boolean value *false* becomes equivalent to the value *0*. You can also see that the Boolean value *true* becomes equivalent to the other non-zero integers.

Arithmetic Operators

Operators	Descriptions
Addition (+)	It adds the operands.
Subtraction (-)	It subtracts the second operand from the previous one.
Multiplication (*)	It multiples both operands.
Division (/)	It divides the first operand by the second operand.
Modulus (%)	It divides the first operand by the second operand and returns the remainder.
Increment Operator (++)	It increases the integer value by one.
Decrement Operator (--)	It decreases the integer value by one.

Logical Operators

Operators	Descriptions
&&	It is the logical AND operator. In the event that both operands are non-zero, the condition is true.
||	It is the logical OR operator. If at least one operand is non-zero, the condition is true.
!	It is the logical NOT operator. It reverses the operand's logical state. In case the condition is found to be true, this operator makes it false.

Bitwise Operators

Operators	Descriptions
& (binary AND)	It copies the bit if it's in both operands.
| (binary OR)	It copies the bit if it is present in either operand.
^ (binary XOR)	It copies the bit if it is present in only one operand.

~ (binary ones complement)	It flips bits.
<< (binary left shift)	It moves the value of the left operand towards the left based on the number of bits assigned by the right operand.
>> (binary right shift)	It moves the value of the left operand towards the right based on the quantity of bits the right operand has assigned.

Misc Operators

Operators	Descriptions
sizeof (sizeof operator)	It returns the size of the variable.
condition ? x : y (conditional operator)	If the condition is found to be true, it returns the value of x. Otherwise, it returns the value of y.
, (comma operator)	It causes a series of operations to be done. Whatever the value of the whole comma expression is, it is also the value of the last expression of the comma-separated list.
. and -> (member	These operators are basically a dot and an arrow. They reference the individual members of unions, classes, and

operators)	structures.
cast (casting operators)	They convert a data type into another.
&	This pointer operator returns the variable's address.
*	This pointer operator is actually a pointer to the variable.

Chapter 6: Statements and Expressions

Statements

A program is basically a series of commands run according to a sequence. In C++, statements control the execution of such sequence. It also does the following: evaluate the expressions, and sometimes, do nothing at all. The null statement is an example of this. All statements, including the null statement, must end with a semicolon.

```
w = x + y ;
```

In the example shown above, you can tell that "*the value of the sum of x and y is assigned to w.*" Take note that this is not the same as in algebra wherein you read it as *w equals x + y*. In C++, assignment operators assign whatever elements are on the right with whatever elements are on the left.

Expressions

Expressions return values. They are also statements.

PI value 3.14	// It is a float const that returns the
3.2	// It returns the value 3.2
SecondsPerMinute the value 60	// It is an inst const that returns

In the given example, *PI* is a constant that is equivalent to *3.14* while *SecondsPerMinute* is another constant that is equivalent to *60*. These three statements are all expressions.

```
y = w + d ;
```

The above sample code is also an expression. It adds w and d, as well as allocates the resulting value to y. It also returns the value of the assignment.

```
w = d = x + y;
```

The code is evaluated from x to y. The resulting value is assigned to d, which in turn is assigned to w. If w, d, x, and y are integers, and x has a value of *3* while y has a value of 7, both w and d will be assigned with the value of *10*.

If you want to find out how you can evaluate complex expressions, you should study the following program:

```
1 : // ***************************************
2 : // This is an evaluation of a complex expression.
3 : # include < iostream.h >
4 : int main ( )
5 : {
6 : int a = 0 , b = 0 , x = 0 , 7 = 35 ;
7 : cout << " a : " << a << " b : " << b ;
8 : cout << " x : " << x << " y : " << y << endl ;
9 : a = 9 ;
10 : b = 7 ;
11 : y = x = a + b ;
12 : cout << " a : " << a << " b : " << b ;
13 : cout << " x : " << x << " y : " << y << endl ;
14 : return 0 ;
15 : }
```

If you run the given sample program, you will get the following output:

```
a : 0   b : 0   x : 0    y : 35
a : 9   b : 7   x : 16   y : 16
```

53

On the sixth line, four variables were initialized and declared. Their corresponding values are shown on the seventh and eighth lines. On the eleventh line, the values of a and b are added and the resulting value is allocated to x. The expression $x = a + b$ evaluates to a value, which is from the sum of $a + b$, and is then allocated to y.

Decision-Making Statements

As a programmer, you need to specify at least one condition for program testing or evaluation in your decision-making structures. You should also include at least one statement for execution in case the condition is found to be true. You may include optional statements in case the condition proves to be otherwise.

Here is the flow diagram of the general form of a decision-making structure:

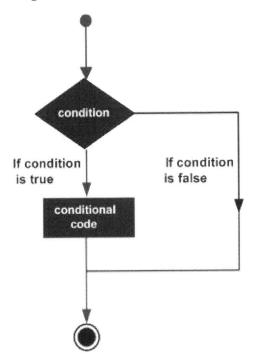

The flow diagram of a decision-making structure is clear and easy to understand. In C++, the following types of decision making statements are used:

Statements	Descriptions
if statement	It consists of a Boolean expression and at least one more statement.
if . . . else statement	It is followed by an optional else statement that executes if a Boolean expression is found to be false.
switch statement	It lets a variable be tested for equality against a set of values.
nested if statement	You are only allowed to use a single if or else if statement within another if or else statement.
nested switch statement	You are allowed to use a switch statement within another switch statement.

The If Statement

It consists of a Boolean expression, which is followed by at least one more statement. Its syntax is as follows:

```
if ( Boolean expression )
{
// This statement will be executed if the Boolean expression is
found to be true.
}
```

The expression inside the parentheses may be any expression. If the expression has a value of 0, it is considered to be false and the statement is ignored. If the value of the expression is non-zero, it is considered to be true and the statement is executed.

If the Boolean expression is found to be true, the block of code within the *if statement* is executed. If it is found to be false, the initial series of code after the end of the *if statement* will be executed.

The flow diagram for the *if statement* is as follows:

Flow Diagram

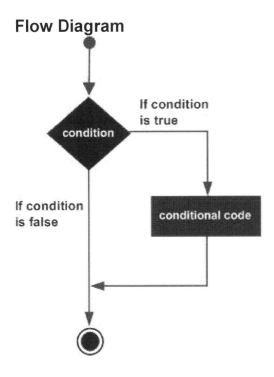

The *if statement* allows you to test for a condition (whether the variables are equal or not, etc.) as well as branch to different areas of your code, based on your resulting output.

```
if ( LargeNumber > SmallNumber )
LargeNumber = SmallNumber ;
```

The sample code above compares the LargeNumber with the SmallNumber. If the LargeNumber is found to be larger indeed, then the second line sets the value to whatever value the SmallNumber has. Since a block of statements with braces is equal to one statement, this type of branch may be large:

```
if ( expression )
{
FirstStatement ;
SecondStatement ;
ThirdStatement ;
}
```

Following the sequence of codes shown above, you can write a program such as the following:

```
if ( LargeNumber > SmallNumber )
{
LargeNumber = SmallNumber ;
cout << "LargeNumber : " << LargeNumber << " \n " ;
cout << "SmallNumber : " << SmallNumber << " \n " ;
}
```

In this case, if LargeNumber is bigger compared to SmallNumber, it would be set to whatever the value of SmallNumber is. Also, an informative message would be printed out.

Here are two other sample programs that make use of the *if statement*:

```
// * * * * * * * * * * * * * * * * * * * * * * * * * * * * * * * * * * * *
* * * * * * * * * *
```

```
// This sample program demonstrates the function of the if statement.
#include < iostream >
using namespace std ;
int main ( )
{
// This is a declaration of a local variable:
int w = 10 ;
// This checks the Boolean condition:
if ( w < 20 )
{
// If the condition is found to be true, the following would be printed:
cout << " w is less than 20 ; " << endl ;
}
cout << " The value of w is : " << w << endl ;
return 0 ;
}
```

If you run the example, you will get the following output:

```
w is less than 20 ;
The value of w is : 10
```

```
1 : // ***********************************************
2 : // This demonstrates the usage of the if statement with relational operators
3 : #include < iostream.h >
4: int main ( )
5 : {
6 : int RedScore , YellowScore ;
7 : cout << "Key in the score for the Red : " ;
8 : cin >> RedScore;
9 :
10 : cout << " \n Key in the score for the Yellow : " ;
11 : cin >> YellowScore ;
```

```
12 :
13 : cout << " \n " ;
14 :
15 : if ( RedScore > YellowScore )
16 : cout << " Go! Go! Go! \n " ;
17 :
18 : if ( RedScore < YellowScore )
19 : {
20 : cout << " Go Yellow ! \n " ;
21 : cout << " Happy days indeed ! \n " ;
22 : }
23 :
24 : if ( RedScore == YellowScore )
25: {
26 : cout << " A tie? Impossible! \n " ;
27 : cout << " Give me the real score for Yellow :  " ;
28 : cin >> YellowScore ;
29 :
30 : if ( RedScore > YellowScore )
31 : cout << " Knew it ! Go Red ! " ;
32 :
33: if ( YellowScore > RedScore )
34: cout << " Knew it ! Go Yellow ! " ;
35:
36: if ( YellowScore == RedScore )
37: cout << " Wow, it really was a tie ! " ;
38: }
39:
40: cout << " \n Thanks for telling me. \n " ;
41: return 0 ;
42: }
```

If you run the given program, you will get the following:

```
Key in the score for the Red : 10
Key in the score for the Yellow : 10
A tie? Impossible!
Give me the real score for Yellow : 8
```

Knew it ! Go Red !
Thanks for telling me.

The program asks you to enter the scores of both Red and Yellow teams. The values of these scores are stored in the integer variables. Then, they are compared with the *if statement* on the fifteenth, eighteenth, and twenty-fourth lines.

If a score is found to be higher than the other, the program prints an informative message. If both scores are found to be equal, the block of code starting on the twenty-fourth line and ending on the thirty-eighth line is entered. The program requests for the second score once more and then compares it with the other given score.

If the first score was found to be higher than the second one, the *if statement* on the fifteenth line would be evaluated to *false* and the sixteenth line would not be invoked. The test on the eighteenth line would be evaluated to *true* and the statements on the twentieth to twenty-first lines would be invoked. The *if statement* on the twenty-fourth line would also be tested. It would evaluate to *false* if ever the eighteenth line was found to be *true*. The whole program would ignore the whole block and fall through to the thirty-ninth line.

Else

If you want your code to be more readable, you should use the keyword *else*. Its syntax is as follows:

```
if ( expression )
statement ;
else
statement ;
```

To understand this concept further, take a look at the following example:

```
1 : // ***************************************
2 : // This demonstrates the usage of the if statement with the else clause
3 : #include < iostream.h >
4 : int main ( )
5 : {
6 : int firstNumber , secondNumber ;
7: cout << " Please enter a big number :  " ;
8 : cin >> firstNumber ;
9 : cout << " \n Please enter a smaller number :  " ;
10 : cin >> secondNumber ;
11 : if ( firstNumber > secondNumber )
12 : cout << " \n Thanks ! \n " ;
13 : else
14 : cout << " \n Oops. The second number is bigger ! " ;
15 :
16 : return 0 ;
17 : }
```

If you run the given program, you would get the following output:

```
Please enter a big number : 10
Please enter a smaller number : 12
Oops. The second number is bigger !
```

On the eleventh line, the *if statement* is evaluated. If the condition is true, the statement on the twelfth line is executed. Otherwise, the statement on the fourteenth line executes. If the *else* clause on the thirteenth line is taken out, the statement on the fourteenth line would still run regardless of the validity of the *if statement*.

61

The *if statement* ends after the twelfth line. If *else* is not found, the fourteenth line would simply be the succeeding line in the program.

Advanced If Statements (Nested If Statements)

You are allowed to use any statement in an *if* or *else* clause, as well as in another *if* or *else* statement. You know that you have complex *if* statements if you see the following format:

```
if ( expression1 )
{
if ( expression2 )
statement ;
else
{
if ( expression3 )
statement2 ;
else
statement3 ;
}
}
else
statement4 ;
```

If both first and second expressions are true, the first statement is executed. If the first and third expressions are true and the second expression is not, the second statement is executed. If the first expression is true, but the second and third expressions are false, the third statement is executed. Finally, if the first expression is false, the fourth statement is executed.

```
#include < iostream >
using namespace std ;
```

```
int main ( )
{
// This is a local variable declaration :
int a = 100 ;
int b = 200 ;
// It checks the Boolean condition
if ( a == 100 )
{
// If the condition is true, then check the following :
if ( b == 200 )
{
// If the condition is true, then the following is printed :
cout << " The value of a is 100 and b is 200 " << endl ;
}
}
cout << " The exact value of a is : " << a << endl ;
cout << " The exact value of b is : " << b << endl ;
return 0 ;
}
```

When the above code is compiled and executed, it produces the following result:

```
The value of a is 100 and b is 200
The exact value of a is : 100
The exact value of b is : 200
```

Nested If Statements and Braces

You should be careful when you nest *if* statements:

```
if ( a > b )          // If a is found to be bigger than b
```

```
if ( a < c )            // and if a is found to be smaller than c
a = b ;                 // then you should set a to the value of c
```

Do not inadvertently assign *else* statements to the incorrect *if* statements. You should also use whitespaces and indentions to make your programs more organized and easier to read.

```
1 : // * * * * * * * * * * * * * * * * * * * * * * * * * * * * * * * * * * * * * * *
2 : // This demonstrates the importance of braces in nested if statements
3 : #include < iostream.h >
4 : int main ( )
5 : {
6 : int x ;
7 : cout << " Enter a number less than 10 or greater than 100 : " ;
8 : cin >> x ;
9 : cout << " \n " ;
10 :
11 : if ( x > 10 )
12 : if ( x > 100 )
13 : cout << " More than 100 , Thanks ! \n " ;
14 : else // not the else intended !
15 : cout << " Less than 10 , Thanks ! \n " ;
16 :
17 : return 0 ;
18 : }
```

If you run this program, you will get the following output:

Enter a number less than 10 or greater than 100 : 20
Less than 10 , Thanks !

The program asked you to enter a number between 10 and 100. When you enter a number, the program checks its value and compares it with the statements before printing a thank you note.

If the *if* statement on the eleventh line is found to be true, the statement on the twelfth line is executed. The twelfth line executes if you enter a number that is greater than 10. The twelfth line contains an *if* statement too, and it evaluates *true* if you enter a number that is greater than 100. Otherwise, the statement on the thirteenth line is executed.

If you enter a number that is less than or equal to 10, then the *if* statement on the tenth line evaluates to *false*. The program moves on to the succeeding line, which is the sixteenth line in the sample program. If you enter a number that is less than 10, you would get the following output:

Enter a number less than 10 or greater than 100 : 9

The *else* clause on the fourteenth line is meant to be attached to the *if* statement on the eleventh line. Because of this, it is indented as necessary. The *else* statement is actually attached to the *if* statement on the twelfth line. Thus, you can say that this program has a bug.

Do not worry because its implications are minimal. Your program is still valid even if it does no function as intended. You can still fix this problem and make your program work the way you wanted to. You just have to put braces and put them in their right places.

```
1 : // ************************************
2 : // This demonstrates the proper use of braces within a nested if statement
3 : #include < iostream.h >
4 : int main ( )
5 : {
6 : int x ;
```

```
7 : cout << " Enter a number less than 10 or greater than 100 : ";
8 : cin >> x ;
9 : cout << " \n " ;
10 :
11 : if ( x > 10 )
12 : {
13 : if ( x > 100 )
14 : cout << " More than 100 , Thanks ! \n " ;
15 : }
16 : else // not the else intended !
17 : cout << " Less than 10 , Thanks ! \n " ;
18 : return 0 ;
19 : }
```

If you run the program, you will get the following output:

Enter a number less than 10 or greater than 100 : 20

The braces are placed on the twelfth and fifteenth lines. They group together all the statements between them. They basically combine these individual statements into just one statement.

The *else* keyword on the sixteenth line applies to the *if* keyword on the eleventh line, as intended. When you type in 20, the program checks the value and verifies that the statement on the eleventh line is *true*. On the other hand, if the *if* statement on the thirteenth line is *false*, nothing shows up.

In order for you to catch errors and be able to print out a message, you should place another *else* clause after the fourteenth line.

The If . . . Else Statement

If statements may sometimes be followed by *else* statements, which execute if the Boolean expressions are found to be false. The *if . . . else statement* has the following syntax:

```
if ( Boolean_expression )
{
// The statement executes if the Boolean expression is found to be true
}
else
{
// The statement executes if the Boolean expression is found to be false
}
```

If the Boolean expression is found to be *true*, the *if block* of code is executed. If not, the *else block* of code is the one that is executed. The flow diagram of the *if . . . else statement* is as follows:

Flow Diagram

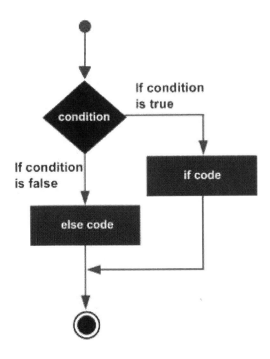

Here is an example of a program that demonstrates the use of an if . . . else statement:

```
#include < iostream >
using namespace std ;
int main ( )
{
// This is a local variable declaration :
int a = 100 ;
// This is to check the Boolean condition :
if ( a < 20 )
{
// If the condition is found to be true, then the following has to be printed :
cout << " a is less than 20 ; " << endl ;
}
else
{
```

```
// If the condition is found to be false, then the following has
to be printed :
cout << " a is not less than 20 ; " << endl ;
}
cout << " The value of a is : " << a << endl ;
return 0 ;
}
```

If you run the above given example, you will get the following output:

```
a is not less than 20 ;
The value of a is : 100
```

The If . . . Else If . . . Else Statement

If statements may be followed by *else if . . . else* statements, which are highly useful when it comes to testing a variety of conditions using the single *if . . . else* if statement. Each time you use an *if . . . else if . . . else* statement, see to it that you remember the following pointers:

- The if statement can have 0 or 1 else statement that has to come after else if.
- The if statement can have 0 or as many else if statements that have to go prior to the else.
- When an else if statement succeeds, no other else if or else would be tested.

The *if . . . else if . . . else* statement has the following syntax:

```
if ( first Boolean expression )
{
// It executes when the first Boolean expression is true
```

```
}
else if ( second Boolean expression )
{
// It executes when the second Boolean expression is true
}
else if ( third Boolean expression )
{
// It executes when the third Boolean expression is true
}
else
{
// It executes when none of the above conditions is true.
}
```

Take a look at the following sample program:

```
#include < iostream >
using namespace std ;
int main ( )
{
// This is a local variable declaration :
int a = 100;
// This is to check the Boolean condition :
if ( a == 10 )
{
// If the condition is found to be true, then the following is printed :
cout << " The value of a is 10 " << endl ;
}
else if ( a == 20 )
{
// If the else if condition is found to be true, then the following is printed :
cout << " The value of a is 20 " << endl ;
}
else if ( a == 30 )
{
```

```
// If the else if condition is found to be true, then the following
is printed :
cout << " The value of a is 30 " << endl ;
}
else
{
// If none of the conditions is found to be true, then the
following is printed :
cout << " The value of a is not matching " << endl ;
}
cout << " The exact value of a is :  " << a << endl ;
return 0 ;
}
```

If you run this, you will get the following output:

```
The value of a is not matching
The exact value of a is : 100
```

The Nested Switch Statement

You can use a switch as part of an outer switch's statement sequence. There are at least two-hundred-and-fifty-six levels of nesting allowed for switch statements. Anyway, the nested switch statement has the following syntax:

```
switch(ch1) {
case 'A':
cout << "This A is part of outer switch";
switch(ch2) {
case 'A':
cout << "This A is part of inner switch";
break;
case 'B': // ...
}
```

```
break;
case 'B': // ...
}
```

Consider the following sample program:

```
#include < iostream >
using namespace std ;
int main ( )
{
// This is a local variable declaration :
int x = 150 ;
int y = 250 ;
switch ( x ) {
case 150 :
cout << " This is part of the outer switch " << endl ;
switch ( y ) {
case 250:
cout << " This is part of the inner switch " << endl ;
}
}
cout << " The exact value of x is :  " << x << endl ;
cout << " The exact value of y is :  " << y << endl ;
return 0 ;
}
```

If you run the program above, you will obtain the following output:

```
This is part of the outer switch
This is part of the inner switch
The exact value of x is : 150
The exact value of y is : 250
```

The Switch Statement

The *switch* statement lets variables be tested for their equality. Every value is referred to as a case. The variable that is switched on is verified for every case.

```
switch ( expression )
{
case constant – expression :
statement ( s ) ;
break ; // This is optional
case constant – expression :
statement ( s ) ;
break ; // This is optional
// You are free to use any number of case statements
default : // This is optional
statement ( s ) ;
}
```

Whenever you use a *switch* statement, see to it that you keep the following pointers in mind:

- All expressions used in switch statements should have an enumerated or integral type.

- Any number of case statements can be used within a switch. Make sure that you follow every case with a value that you compare it with, as well as a colon.

- Make sure that you use a constant (same data type as that of your switch's variable). It has to be a literal or a constant.

- If the variable you switch on is equivalent to a case, all statements that follow such case would be executed until the program reaches a break statement.

- Once the program reaches a break statement, it terminates the switch and the control flow moves on to the line that follows the switch statement.

- You do not need to use a break all the time. If you do not see a break, the control flow falls through to the next cases until the program reaches a break statement.

- You can also use a default case in a switch statement. It is optional, so you can skip it. If you decide to use one, make sure that you put it at the switch's end.

The flow diagram of a switch statement is as follows:

Flow Diagram

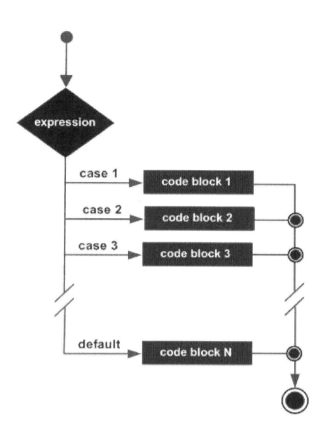

Chapter 7: Arrays

Arrays are collections of data storage locations that hold the same class of data. A storage location is referred to as an *element of the array*. You can declare arrays by identifying and writing their type, name, and subscript.

Subscripts are the numbers of elements in an array. They involve square brackets. Say, if you input the following:

```
long LongArray [ 20 ] ;
```

The statement makes a declaration of an array of 20 long integers and is named LongArray. Once the compiler reads this, it immediately prepares the memory to hold these twenty elements. Since every long integer needs four bytes, this particular declaration prepares one hundred contiguous bytes of memory.

Elements of an Array

All elements of an array can be accessed through their name's offset. These elements get counted, starting from zero. Thus, the first element of an array is ArrayName [0] .

If you use LongArray, your first array element would be LongArray [0] ; your second array element would be LongArray [1] , and so on.

SomeArray [3] , for example, is an array that contains three elements, namely SomeArray [0] , SomeArray [1] , and SomeArray [2] . Moreover, SomeArray [n] contains numbered elements from SomeArray [0] until SomeArray [n – 1] . So, LongArray [25] is numbered from LongArray [0] until LongArray [24] .

```
1 : // ***************************************
2 : // This is a demonstration of the use of an integer array
3 : #include < iostream.h >
4 :
5 : int main ( )
6 : {
7 : int myArray [ 5 ] ;
8 : int i ;
9 : for ( i = 0; i < 5; i + + )          // This counts from 0 to 4
10 : {
11 : cout << "The value for myArray [ " << i << " ] : " ;
12 : cin >> myArray [ i ] ;
13 : }
14 : for ( i = 0 ; i < 5 ; i + + )
15 : cout << i << " : " << myArray [ i ] << " \n " ;
16 : return 0 ;
17 : }
```

If you run the given program, you will obtain the following output:

```
The value for myArray[0]: 3
The value for myArray[1]: 6
The value for myArray[2]: 9
The value for myArray[3]: 12
The value for myArray[4]: 15
0: 3
1: 6
2: 9
3: 12
4: 15
```

On the seventh line, you can see a declaration of an array named myArray. It has five integer variables. On the ninth line, a loop counting from 0 to 4 is established. This set of offsets is just right for an array with five elements. You are then prompted to input a value, which is eventually saved at the right offset into your array.

The first value you entered is saved to myArray [0] while the second value you entered is saved to myArray [1] . All your other values are saved to their corresponding arrays. These values are then printed to your screen by the second *for* loop.

Arrays generally begin at 0, not at 1. If you start at 1, your program will have a bug and it will not run properly. Remember that an array that contains ten elements should count from ArrayName [0] to ArrayName [9]. Do not include ArrayName [10] .

Writing Past the End of Arrays

When you input values to the elements of an array, your compiler calculates where it should store them. It considers their sizes and subscripts.

For example, if you want to write over a value stored at LongArray [5] , you can expect your compiler to multiply the offset according to the size of every element. Here, these values are 5 and 4, respectively. It also moves 20 bytes from the start of your array and writes the new values on that same location.

If you wish to write at LongArray [50] , your compiler will compute how far past your first element is. It will then write over any value on that particular location. Writing the new value may cause you to gain unpredictable outputs.

```
1 : // *******************************************
2 : // This is a demonstration of what occurs when you write past the end of an array.
```

```
3: #include < iostream.h >
4 : int main ( )
5 : {
6 : // These are sentinels :
7 : long sentinelOne [ 3 ] ;
8 : long TargetArray [ 25 ] ; // This is an array to fill
9 : long sentinelTwo [ 3 ] ;
10 : int i ;
11 : for ( i = 0 ; i < 3 ; i + + )
12 : sentinelOne [ i ] = sentinelTwo [ i ] = 0 ;
13 :
14 : for ( i = 0 ; i < 25 ; i + + )
15 : TargetArray [ i ] = 0 ;
16 :
17 : cout << " Test 1 : \n " ;   // This tests the current values (
These values have to be 0 )
18 : cout << " TargetArray [ 0 ] :  " << TargetArray [ 0 ] << "
\n " ;
19 : cout << " TargetArray [24 ] : " << TargetArray [ 24 ] << "
\n \n " ;
20 :
21 : for ( i = 0 ; i < 3 ; i + + )
22 : {
23 : cout << " sentinelOne [ " << i << " ] :  " ;
24 : cout << sentinelOne [ i ] << " \n " ;
25 : cout << " sentinelTwo [ " << i << " ] :  " ;
26 : cout << sentinelTwo [ i ]<< " \n " ;
27 : }
28 :
29 : cout << " \n Assigning . . . " ;
30 : for ( i = 0 ; i <= 25 ; i + + )
31 : TargetArray [ i ] = 20 ;
32 :
33 : cout << " \n Test 2 : \n " ;
34 : cout << " TargetArray [ 0 ] :  " << TargetArray [ 0 ] << "
\n " ;
35 : cout << " TargetArray [ 24 ] :  " << TargetArray [ 24 ] << "
\n " ;
```

```
36 : cout << " TargetArray [ 25 ] : " << TargetArray [ 25 ] << " \n\ n ";
37 : for ( i = 0 ; i <3 ; i + + )
38 : {
39 : cout << " sentinelOne [ " << i << " ] : ";
40 : cout << sentinelOne [ i ] << " \n ";
41 : cout << " sentinelTwo [ " << i << " ] : ";
42 : cout << sentinelTwo [ i ] << " \n ";
43 : }
44 :
45 : return 0 ;
46 : }
```

If you run the given example, you would get the following output:

```
Test 1 :
TargetArray [ 0 ] : 0
TargetArray [ 24 ] : 0
SentinelOne [ 0 ] : 0
SentinelTwo [ 0 ] : 0
SentinelOne [ 1 ] : 0
SentinelTwo [ 1 ] : 0
SentinelOne [ 2 ] : 0
SentinelTwo [ 2 ] : 0
Assigning ...
Test 2 :
TargetArray [ 0 ] : 20
TargetArray [ 24 ] : 20
TargetArray [ 25 ] : 20
SentinelOne [ 0 ] : 20
SentinelTwo [ 0 ] : 0
SentinelOne [ 1 ] : 0
SentinelTwo [ 1 ] : 0
SentinelOne [ 2 ] : 0
SentinelTwo [ 2 ] : 0
```

Should you run this sample program? No, you should not. If you do, it will just crash. You will not get any useful result from it.

On the seventh and eighth lines of the program, two arrays that are of three integers which function as sentinels on TargetArray are declared. They are initialized with the value of 0 and are most likely to be changed if the memory is made to go past the end of the TargetArray.

On the seventeenth to twenty-seventh lines, the values in Test 1 are confirmed. On the thirty-first line, all the members in TargetArray are initialized to the value of 20. However, the counter still counts to TargetArray and offset twenty-five, which does not exist in the TargetArray.

On the thirty-fourth to thirty-eighth lines, the values of TargetArray in Test 2 are printed. TargetArray [25] is very much willing to display the value 20. Then again, when SentinelOne and SentinelTwo gets printed, SentinelTwo [0] shows that the value has been modified.

Array Initialization

When you first declare an array, you may initialize it as a simple array, like characters and integers. Do not forget an equal sign (=) and a series of values that are separated by commas. Of course, you have to enclose all of these in braces.

Consider the following sample code:

```
int IntegerArray [ 5 ] = { 10, 20, 30, 40, 50 } ;
```

The IntegerArray is declared as an array that contains five integers. It allocates the value of 10 to IntegerArray [0] and the value of 20 to IntegerArray [1] . The same process of allocating values continues until the last IntegerArray. If you skip the array size, you create an array that is large enough for an initialization.

So, if you input

```
int IntegerArray [ ] = { 10, 20, 30, 40, 50 } ;
```

you create exactly the same array you created before.

If you wish to determine the array size, you can simply ask your compiler to compute it. For instance, you can input the following:

```
const USHORT IntegerArrayLength ;
IntegerArrayLength = sizeof ( IntegerArray ) / sizeof ( IntegerArray [ 0 ] ) ;
```

This code sets the constant USHORT variable IntegerArrayLength to whatever result you get from dividing the whole array size by the individual array size. The quotient you get is the number of array members.

You are not allowed to initialize elements that you have declared for your array. So, if you use the following:

```
int IntegerArray [ 5 ] = { 10, 20, 30, 40, 50, 60 } ;
```

You generate a compiler error. This happens because you declared an array with five members, and yet you initialized six values.

Nonetheless, it is legal to write the following:

```
int IntegerArray [ 5 ] = { 10, 20 } ;
```

Even though uninitialized array members do not have any guaranteed values, the aggregates are still initialized to 0. When you do not initialize your array member, the value would be set to 0.

You have to let your compiler set the initialized array size. You should never write beyond the end part of an array. Just like with variables, see to it that you use sensible names for your arrays. Also, you have to keep in mind that the initial array member is always at offset 0.

Array Declaration

You can choose whatever legal variable name you want for your array. Just refrain from choosing a name that is the same as that of another variable as well as an array within scope. With this being said, you cannot name one particular array *myCat [3]* and another variable *myCat*. You can, however, use *const* or use an enumeration to dimension your array size.

```
1 : // ***************************************
2 : // This shows how to dimension arrays using consts and enumerations.
3 :
4 : #include < iostream.h >
5 : int main ( )
6 : {
7 : enum WeekDays { Sun, Mon, Tue,
8 : Wed, Thu, Fri, Sat, DaysInWeek } ;
9 : int ArrayWeek [ DaysInWeek ] = { 10, 20, 30, 40, 50, 60, 70 } ;
10 :
11 : cout << " The value at Tuesday is :  " << ArrayWeek [ Tue ] ;
12 : return 0 ;
13 : }
```

If you run the sample program shown above, you will get the following output:

The value at Tuesday is: 30

In the sample program above, you can see on the seventh line that an enumeration named *WeekDays* has been created. It has eight members. *DaysInWeek* is equivalent to 7 while *Sunday* is equivalent to 0.

On the eleventh line, an enumerated constant *Tue* is used as an offset into your array. Since *Tue* evaluates to 2, *DaysInWeek [2]*, which is the third element in your array, is returned. It also gets printed on the eleventh line.

When you declare arrays, you should always define the type of object stored, the name of your array, and a subscript that contains the number of objects to be held in such array. Consider the following examples:

int MyIntegerArray [90] ;

long * ArrayOfPointersToLongs [100] ;

If you wish to access the members of an array, you can use the subscript operator, such as in the following examples:

int theNinthInteger = MyIntegerArray [8] ;

long * pLong = ArrayOfPointersToLongs [8]

All arrays count starting at zero. Arrays of *n* items are numbered from 0 to n – 1.

84

Multidimensional Arrays

You can use arrays with more than one dimension in the C++ programming language. Every dimension is represented as an array subscript. This means that a 2-dimensional array has two subscripts and a 3-dimensional array has three. An array can have any number of dimensions. However, it is most likely that you will create an array with 1 or 2 dimensions.

For example, you declared a class called SQUARE. If you declare an array called Cardboard that represents it, you have to write:

SQUARE Cardboard [8] [8] ;

You can also represent this data using a 1-dimensional, 64-square array, such as in the following:

SQUARE Cardboard [64]

Multidimensional Array Initialization

You can initialize multidimensional arrays, as well as assign the list of values to the elements in the array in a certain order. You can do this as the last array subscript changes and every one of the former stays in place. So if you write:

int theArray [5] [3]

You meant for the first three elements to go to theArray [0] and the succeeding ones to theArray [1] and so on.

int theArray [5] [3] = { 1 , 2 , 3 , 4 , 5 , 6 , 7 , 8 , 9 , 10 , 11 , 12 , 13 , 14 , 15 }

To make everything much clearer, you can group your initializations using braces. Consider the following example:

int theArray [5] [3] = { { 1 , 2 , 3 } ,

85

```
{ 4 , 5 , 6 } ,
{ 7 , 8 , 9 } ,
{ 10 , 11 , 12 } ,
{ 13 , 14 , 15 } } ;
```

Keep in mind that these inner braces are ignored by the compiler. So, if you want to make your program more effective, you should use braces instead. They represent the distribution of numbers. Do not forget to use a comma to separate the values, regardless of the braces. Your entire initialization set has to be within the braces. Of course, it has to end with a semicolon.

The following is an example of a program that creates a 2-dimensional array, with the first dimension being a set of numbers from 0 to 5 and the second one consisting of the double of the values of the previous.

```
1 : // ***********************************************
2 : // This shows how to dimension arrays using consts and enumerations.
3 : #include < iostream.h >
4 : int main ( )
5 : {
6 : int SomeArray [ 5 ] [ 2 ] = { { 0 , 0 } , { 1 , 2 } , { 2 , 4 } , { 3 , 6 } , { 4 , 8 } } ;
7 : for ( int i = 0 ; i < 5 ; i + + )
8 : for ( int j = 0 ; j < 2 ; j + + )
9 : {
10 : cout << " SomeArray [ " << i << " ] [ " << j << " ] : " ;
11 : cout << SomeArray [ i ] [ j ] << endl ;
12 : }
13 :
14 : return 0 ;
15 : }
```

If you run the above given program, you will get the following output:

SomeArray [0] [0] : 0
SomeArray [0] [1] : 0
SomeArray [1] [0] : 1
SomeArray [1] [1] : 2
SomeArray [2] [0] : 2
SomeArray [2] [1] : 4
SomeArray [3] [0] : 3
SomeArray [3] [1] : 6
SomeArray [4] [0] : 4
SomeArray [4] [1] : 8

On the sixth line, SomeArray is declared as a 2-dimensional array. On the first dimension, five integers are present. On the contrary, the second dimension has two integers. Because of the presence of these figures, you can have a 5 x 2 grid.

With a 5 x 2 array, all values are initialized by two or in pairs. You may compute them if you want. On the seventh and eighth lines, a nested *for* loop is created. The outer *for* loop goes through every member from the first dimension while the inner *for* loop goes through every member from the second dimension.

You should keep in mind that this is consistent with your printout. Hence, SomeArray [0] [0] precedes SomeArray [0] [1] . The first dimension only gets incremented once the second dimension has been incremented by 1. The second dimension then starts over.

Chapter 8: Case Studies In Terms of Compatibility

The following case studies are done by Bjarne Stroustrup.

It is not easy to make changes in any programming language. In fact, even the simplest changes require considerations and discussions that take a lot of time and effort. More often than not, readers will wonder how the programmer designed his program and made a mess. When this happens, the programmer has to figure out what would break the least code, what would provide the best benefits, how easy it is to recover broken codes, and how complicated it is to implement resolutions.

Variadic Function Syntax

Variadic functions are indicated by commas that are followed by ellipses at the end of arguments. This is in the C language. However, in C++, you can just use ellipses and your program will be just fine.

```
// C language and C++
int printf ( const char * , ... ) ;
// C++
int printf ( const char * ... ) ;
```

In the C language, the plain ellipses have to be accepted. The resolution does not break any code. It does not impose any run time overhead. It even neglects the added compiler complexity. Other resolutions break a lot of code without compensating benefits.

Also, variadic functions are required to have one or more specific arguments in the C language. This is not necessary in

C++. You do not need to specify any argument at all. Consider the following example:

```
void f ( ... );              // C++
```

As you can see, this one suffices in C++ but not in the C language. You can allow the construct in the C language. You can also disallow it in C++. If you opt to allow it in the C language, you will not break any user code. However, you may experience problems when it comes to C implementers. If you choose to go with the latter option, you can break some code, but this code may be obscure and rare. Nevertheless, you can still find ways on how to rewrite it. Between these two options, you should probably adopt the C rule and ban the construct in the C++ programming language.

When it comes to breaking codes, you have to keep in mind that you should never do it lightly. Then again, there are times when it is better to break a code than let a problem go on for a longer period of time. In this case, you have to consider banning constructs as well as using codes to hide errors. In most cases, a compiler easily detects a broken code caused by a change in language.

It is not really that bad to break a code. The diagnosable incompatibility does not have any impact on the compatibility of the link, such as new keyword introduction. It can even be beneficial for the entire community since it reminds users that everything changes constantly. This encourages them to review old codes. Then again, compatibility switches are still necessary to help users get reacquainted with old source codes.

Pointer to Void and Null

Void may be assigned to T without the need for explicit casting. That is in the C language. In C++, however, there is no way you can do this without experiencing any problems. C++ has restrictions when it comes to void. If you are using this programming language, you will find out that converting void to T is not safe. So, even if it is commonly used in the C language, it is not used in C++.

```
// malloc ( ) returns a void *
int * p = malloc ( sizeof ( int ) * n ) ;
// NULL is typically a macro for ( void * ) 0
struct X * p = NULL ;
```

In C++, *malloc* is not advisable to be used in place of *new*. However, programmers commonly use (void *) 0 in the C language, thereby producing an advantage of being able to differentiate nil pointers from plain 0s. Then again, in C++, the Classic C NULL definition has been retained. Likewise, the programming language has maintained the tradition of using plan 0 instead of NULL. If (void *) 0 was used with a pointer, however, it may have been helpful in overloading. Take a look at the following:

```
void f ( int ) ;
void f ( char * ) ;

void g ( )
{
        // 0 is an int, call f ( int )
        f ( 0 ) ;
        // C++ error, why not call f ( char * ) instead
        f ( ( void * ) 0 ;
}
```

As you can see, there is an incompatibility. Nevertheless, there are still ways on how you can resolve this.

Keep in mind that the C rule is accepted in C++ and the C++ rule is accepted in C. Both programming languages ban implicit conversions except for certain cases in the standard library, such as malloc and NULL. Furthermore, the C rule for void * is accepted in C++. Both programming languages also feature a new type, say raw *, which gives safer semantics in C++.

Prototypes

There are no functions that are allowed to be called without being declared first in the C++ programming language. In the C language, however, non-variadic functions are allowed to be called even without previous prototypes. Then again, this is no longer a common practice.

```
int f ( i )
{
        // C++ error, deprecated in the C language
        int x = g ( i ) ;
        // ...
}
```

Every lint and compiler has a mechanism for detecting its use. Keep in mind the following alternatives: calls are allowed (as in the C language, but deprecated) and calls are not allowed to undeclared functions (as in the C++ language).

The second one should be the resolution, as the deprecation represents. If the first one is chosen, the type of checking in the C++ language will be weak and will go against general programming trends without any compensating benefits.

Chapter 9: Quizzes

This chapter is dedicated to quizzes to see if you have really understood C++ and the concept of the programming language.

1. Provide the output for the following code:

```cpp
#include < iostream >
using namespace std ;
int main ( )
{
// This is a local variable declaration :
char grade = ' D ' ;
switch ( grade )
{
case ' A ' :
cout << " Excellent ! " << endl ;
break;
case ' B ' :
case ' C ' :
cout << " Well done " << endl ;
break;
case ' D ' :
cout << " You passed " << endl ;
break;
case ' F ' :
cout << " Better try again " << endl ;
break ;
default :
cout << " Invalid grade " << endl ;
}
cout << " Your grade is " << grade << endl ;
return 0 ;
}
```

2. Provide the output for the following code:

```cpp
#include <string>
#include <iostream>

int main ( )
{
    for (int j = 0; j < 10; ++j)
    {
        std::string a(1, 'w');
        std::cout << a << std::endl;
    }
    return 0;
}
```

```cpp
#include <string>
#include <iostream>

int main ( )
{
    for (int j = 0; j < 10; ++j)
    {
        std::string a(1, 'w');
        std::cout << a << '\n';
    }
    return 0;
}
```

3. Provide the output for the following code:

```cpp
#include <iostream>
int main (void)

{
    std::cout << " First Output" << std::endl;
    std::cout << "Second Output \n";
```

}

4. What happens when you write the element 25 in a 24-member array?

5. Is it possible to combine arrays? Explain your answer.

6. Which one is more efficient: using built-in arrays or creating array classes? Explain your answer.

7. When you use tabs, new lines, and spaces, what happens to your program?

8. What are negative numbers? Are they true or false?

9. How many times does a do loop get executed at the minimum?

10. What do you call variables that can only be used within the function wherein it was declared?

11. What is the number of values that a function can return?

12. What do you call variables that represent individual array elements in arrays?

13. What do you call variables that contain the address of other variables?

14. What does int stand for in int main ( ) ?

15. What does endl do to the program?

16. What is <iostream>

17. Which of the following should you use if you want to print to your screen?

a. cin << "Hello world << endl ;

b. cout << "Hello world" << endl ;

c. cout << ("Hello world) ;

18. In which memory segment are machine instructions stored?

19. What is the complete form of STL?

20. Provide the output for the following code:

```
#include <iostream>
using namespace std;

void f ( )
{
        static int i;

        ++i;
cout << i << " ";
}

main ( )
{
        f();
        f();
        f();
}
```

Conclusion

Thank you again for reading this book!

I hope this book was able to help you learn how to program using C++.

The next step is to apply what you have learned from this book and be a good programmer.

Finally, if you enjoyed this book, then I'd like to ask you for a favor, would you be kind enough to leave a review for this book on Amazon? It'd be greatly appreciated!

Thank you and good luck!

Made in the USA
San Bernardino, CA
12 March 2017